D1621560

Deep in the Amazon

NATIVE PEOPLES

Ancient and effective, the blowgun has been used for centuries. First developed in Southeast Asia, it is uncertain if the weapon was introduced to South America or reinvented by the continent's native inhabitants.

Deep in the Amazon

NATIVE PEOPLES

by James L. Castner

BENCHMARK BOOKS

MARSHALL CAVENDISH
NEW YORK

*With thanks to Dr. Gary Hartshorn, Organization for Tropical Studies,
Duke University, for his careful review of the manuscript.*

Benchmark Books
Marshall Cavendish Corporation
99 White Plains Road
Tarrytown, New York 10591-9001
www.marshallcavendish.com

• • •

Library of Congress Cataloging-in-Publication Data
Castner, James L.
Native Peoples / James L. Castner
p. cm—(Deep in the Amazon)
Includes bibliographical references (p.).
ISBN 0-7614-1128-3
1. Indians of South America—Amazon River Valley—Juvenile literature.
2. Ethnology—Amazon River Valley—Juvenile Literature.   3. Amazon River Valley—
Social life and customs—Juvenile literature.   [1. Indians of South America—Amazon River Valley.
2. Amazon River Valley—Social life and customs.]   I. Title
F2519. 1.A6 C37 2001   981'.1—dc21   00-052940

• • •

Printed in Hong Kong
1 3 5 7 8 6 4 2

• • •

Book Designer: Judith Turziano
Photo Research: Candlepants Incorporated

• • •

CREDITS
Cover photo: Loren McIntyre
The photographs in this book are used by permission and through the courtesy of;
Loren McIntyre, 23, 8, 10, 12, 14, 16, 17, 18, 20, 21, 22, 24, 28, 48, 52, 54 (lower), 58;
Dr. James L. Castner, 27, 43, 44, 47, 50, 54 (top); *DDBStock Photos:* Nair Benedicto, 30, 40; J. Rippen
Stock Photos, 36; Art Wolfe, 32, 56; *Photo Researchers Inc.:* Victor Englebert, 34, 35; Carl Frank, 38, 39.

CONTENTS

CARIBBEAN SEA

GUYANA

SURINA

VENEZUELA

○ Bogotá

SIERRA PARIMA
MOUNTAINS

COLOMBIA

YANOMAMI

Negro River

Equator

Putumayo River

ECUADOR

SHUAR

Napo R.

YAGUA

Manaus ○

Iquitos ○

Amazon River

Tapajós River

SHIPIBO

Leticia ○

Marañón River

Ucayali River

Madeira River

BRAZIL

Pucallpa ○

PERU

ANDES MOUNTAINS

BOLIVIA

PACIFIC OCEAN

Four Native Homelands

(locations are approximate)

0   400 miles

0   600 kilometers

AUTHOR'S NOTE

As a frequent visitor to the Amazon rain forest, I am frequently awed by the strange, often spectacular plants and animals that I come across. And with good reason. For nowhere else on Earth do life-forms occur in such abundance and variety.

But to better understand the rain forest we must take a look at the groups that first called the region home. People have been adapting to life in the Amazon Basin for more than 12,000 years. They have formed an ancient partnership with the land that has fed, clothed, and housed them. But too often we must use the past tense in speaking of these vibrant cultures. The Amazon River basin has changed much since the days when people first settled here. It is an area rich in natural resources and thus has been the target of countless people who have come to harvest and extract its wealth.

Hundreds of native groups make their home in the basin. There is no way to do justice to each, so I have chosen four. Like all the Amazon's original residents, they have struck a balance with the natural world. Today, however, they must strike a similar balance with the modern world that constantly closes in around them. Despite grave challenges, theirs is a story of survival.

Amazon Indians fashioned
their tools and weapons from
the materials supplied by the
surrounding forest. They were
made from wood, bone,
bamboo, and stone
when available. Here,
a man puts the finishing
touches on a spear point.

Chapter One

THE GREAT MIGRATION

W ho were the original inhabitants of the Amazon Basin? Where did they come from? To help answer these questions we must look into the past at a series of geological events. From 1.6 million years ago to 11,000 B.C., the earth experienced a great ice age. Thick sheets of ice covered northern Europe and Asia and North America as far south as the Great Lakes. With so much of Earth's water frozen in the ice sheets, the levels of the oceans were much lower than they are today. The extreme climate produced important changes in the look and shape of the land. In the Amazon Basin, the rain forest shrunk to a series of isolated pockets known as refugia. These patches of trees thrived in only the wettest areas.

Today, the west coast of Alaska is separated from Russia by a strip of water called the Bering Strait. However, during the ice age, when massive glaciers formed in the north, the oceans receded, revealing the land beneath the Bering Strait. Over this land bridge that now connected the two continents, bands of humans began to migrate from Asia to North America. They may have also traveled in boats along the northern Pacific coast. These people were hunter-gatherers who followed game animals and harvested whatever edible plants, fruits, and nuts they could find. Countless groups of Paleo-Indians filtered into the New World some time between 40,000 and 20,000 years ago.

No one knows how long it took these migrating bands to make their

Although the descendants of the basin's original residents still inhabit the region today, many native groups have died out or become acculturated. Over the course of his lifetime, this Yagua elder has witnessed great shifts in the daily life of his people.

way down the North American continent to South America. Archaeological evidence suggests that humans had reached the Isthmus of Panama 15,000 years ago and had settled in and spread throughout the Amazon region by 12,000 years ago. The habitat at that time was mostly savannah and grassland, as the rain forests were still confined to clusters of refugia. But as the ice age drew to a close, all this was to change. As the climate gradually warmed and the rain forests spread once again, humans were forced to adapt to their slowly changing environment.

European Arrivals

By the time the first European explorers reached the Amazon Basin in the 1500s, there were an estimated six million people living throughout the lowlands. These descendants of the original settlers lived in groups scattered throughout the vast forest. While their beliefs, customs, and languages varied, these people shared one common bond. They had all learned to survive in the rain forest.

Unfortunately, contact with European civilizations had a devastating effect on the Indian populations of the Amazon. Considered savages without rights, they were abused and enslaved by the colonizing powers of Spain, Portugal, Great Britain, France, and Holland. The Europeans also brought with them diseases against which the Indians had no resistance. Illnesses such as the measles were fatal and killed thousands. In the late 1800s during the rubber boom, the native inhabitants were forced to harvest latex from trees growing in the forest. Thousands were tortured and died performing this physically demanding work.

By 1900, it is estimated that only one million Indians remained in more than 200 separate tribes. By 1960, more than 80 of these tribes had disappeared completely. Today, probably no more than 200,000 natives remain. In a region where now almost no one can be completely isolated, most have become acculturated — their customs and traditions replaced by those of the modern world. Still, some cultures do persist and are fighting to retain both the land where they live and their beliefs.

For centuries, the Shuar have lived in the mountainous forests of eastern Ecuador.

Chapter Two

THE SHUAR

*T*he Shuar (SHOO-arr), sometimes called the Jívaro (HEE-var-oh), is one of the few tribal groups to have successfully resisted the efforts of rivals and foreign powers to conquer them. Even the mighty Inca empire, which ruled a population of more than 12 million in the fifteenth and early sixteenth centuries, could not bring the Shuar under its control. The Shuar homeland sits on what were once rich gold deposits. The Spaniards managed to gain a foothold in the territory in the late 1500s. Driven to extract as much gold as possible, their greed and merciless taxation of the Shuar led to a massive revolt. This uprising took place in 1599, when the Shuar banded together to free themselves of Spanish rule. They captured, tortured, and executed the Spanish governor of the region and then slaughtered most of the 20,000 Spanish settlers in the area.

The strength and skill of their warriors helped the Shuar stay independent for so long. But the location of their homeland was another important reason as well. The Shuar live in an area of mountainous rain forests in eastern Ecuador. The foothills of the towering Andes mountain chain form their western border. The other boundaries are formed by rivers filled with dangerous rapids, making them difficult or impossible to navigate. Nature served the Shuar well to isolate them from the advances of conquistadors, explorers, and settlers who would not be halted elsewhere. Thus they remained unchallenged for more than three hundred years in their mist-shrouded forest homes. It was not until the nineteenth century that morbid curiosity and a genuine cultural interest brought this group out of the shadows. Anthropologist Michael Harner, who lived with the Shuar in the 1950s and the 1960s, was one of the first people to study them seriously. He called them the "people of the sacred waterfalls."

The Shuar live in villages that are actually loose clusters of five to six households spread throughout the same area. Each household is occupied by a single family group, which seldom builds near its neighbors, unless they are close relatives. The dwellings are built on high ground, deep inside the forest and usually near a stream. The area around the house is cultivated into a garden. Manioc, corn, beans, squash, and tobacco are commonly seen growing in the carefully tended plots. The house itself stands like a fortress, large and oval shaped, and usually measures 40 to 60 feet (12–18 m) long by 20 to 30 feet (6–9 m) wide. The outer, windowless walls consist of closely spaced poles of palm, with just

Today, Shuar settlements are structured much like they were in the past. Neighborhoods were once formed around the household of a "great man," a position of prominence in Shuar society reserved for warriors who had distinguished themselves in battle.

enough room between them for light and air to enter. The roof is made of tightly woven palm thatch. There is a door at either end of the house, one for men and one for women. A house is typically lived in for five to six years, even though it could be occupied for much longer. By then however, the residents have used up much of the local firewood supply, and the family moves on in search of new sources of food as well.

A typical household consists of from five to ten people, depending on the number of children and whether a man has one or more wives. Other family members and relatives may also be permanent residents. Each sex has their own side of the house and their own duties. The man is the head of the household and responsible for protecting the women and children. Men do the heavy labor required to clear areas of the forest for gardens. They also cut and haul firewood and do the hunting and fishing. Women are responsible for almost all other tasks, including tending the children, the livestock, and the garden. Most men have two wives as this increases food production since the women perform all agricultural duties. It also means that one wife can accompany him when he hunts and help him to carry back game that has been killed.

Making manioc beer, or *chicha*, is another important duty for Shuar women. To brew the beverage, the manioc root is peeled, washed, then boiled. Once it is soft, it is mashed. During this process, the women add a special ingredient. They chew pieces of manioc root and then spit them into the mixture. While this seems less than appealing, it is an essential step in preparing the beer. The chemicals in the saliva allow the beer to ferment more quickly, usually in four to five days. Then the beverage, a Shuar favorite, is enjoyed by the entire family.

Head Shrinkers

Although the Shuar are well known for their beer-making technique, their fame spread for another reason. They removed and shrunk the heads of their enemies. Warfare, headhunting, and revenge were accept-

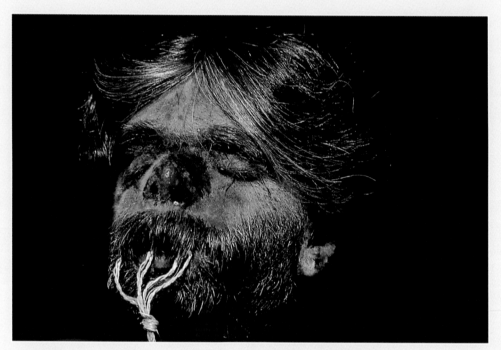

Warfare was once a central part of Shuar life. Their practice of shrinking heads made them one of the basin's most feared groups. To a Shuar warrior, head shrinking not only prevented vengeance, it was a way for him to acquire power from the spirit of his enemy.

ed ways of life for the Shuar. Enemy households were often raided by war parties and their inhabitants slain. The threat posed by an enemy warrior did not die with his body, however. To eliminate the desire for revenge from the dead warrior's soul, the Shuar decapitated the victim and set about reducing the size of his head. The process involved removing the skin and scalp from the skull, sewing the lips and eyelids shut, and boiling it. Hot rocks and sand were poured into the hollow head to help it retain its shape and to continue to shrink it by drying out the tissues. After a day or two of preparation, the enemy's head was about one-fourth of its original size, or as big as a man's fist.

Following the completion of the head-shrinking process, a large celebration was held. During this feast, the shrunken head called a *tsantsa* (SAN-sah) was shouted at and insulted. The Shuar believed this would intimidate the spirit and soul of the enemy warrior, so that it would not seek revenge against the victorious Shuar warrior. Once the celebration was over, the *tsantsa* was buried or discarded, its power having been removed.

The Shuar have been the subject of a growing fascination. Since the late 1800s, collectors have sought the mysterious and hard-to-find shrunken heads that have become an emblem of the tribe. But beyond the violence and bloodshed lies an enduring culture that successfully faced the challenges of life in the rain forest. The Shuar's story is one of unity and resistance. In the twentieth century they could not stem the wave of missionaries, miners, and land-hungry settlers. These outsiders swept in and seized much of their holdings, threatening their culture in the process. As pressures increased, the Shuar organized themselves into the Federación de Centros Shuaras in 1964. As one of the oldest and most successful native organizations, the group not only defends Shuar rights, it serves as a model for the Amazon's other native groups.

The Shuar have made great strides in obtaining legal ownership of their territory, ensuring there will be a homeland for future generations.

Like its mother, this Shipibo baby wears a silver nose ornament. The black dye on the baby's forehead is huito, *made from the fruit of the genipap tree.*

Chapter Three

THE SHIPIBO

I n the rain forest that thrives within the Ucayali River basin of east-central Peru exists a native group that has achieved recognition, not as fierce warriors, but as skilled artisans and craftspeople. The Shipibo (shuh-PEE-boh) number more than 25,000 and are found in about 110 scattered settlements and villages north of the city of Pucallpa. Because there are few roads in this dense patch of forest, paddling the region's many rivers is often the most efficient means of travel.

In order to make the best use of the scarce land, the Shipibo do not live in large settlements. Instead their compounds are spread mostly along riverbanks in villages of no more than forty families. Compounds are made up of several dwellings grouped together and used by a single extended family. The main house is an all-purpose room where people sleep and the women spin cotton and weave their textiles. It is built of wooden support poles, with a roof covered in palm leaves. The floor is raised off the ground and made of bark stripped from palm trees. In rare cases, a floor of boards obtained from a sawmill may be built and firmly secured with nails. Typically there are no walls. Mosquito nets, which are stored in the rafters during the day, are brought down for use at night. The married women also have a separate cooking house as part of the compound. Enough distance is left between compounds to ensure a degree of privacy.

This arrangement seems to fit the way the Shipibo view and organize their society. Despite being linked by the same ancestors and speaking the same language, the Shipibo do not consider themselves a nation.

An aerial view of a Shipibo village. Two metal roofs stand out among the row of traditionally thatched dwellings, an example of the ways the outside world has begun to influence native societies.

They do not have a single leader or one official code of law. Each extended family forms a small community and makes its own decisions under the guidance of the men.

Traditionally, the Shipibo had a matriarchal society, which means that the women ran the households and made the important decisions. When a Shipibo couple marries, the man goes to live in his wife's village. They are also matrilineal. Thus the group that inhabits a particular compound traces its descent through the mother's family line. The Shipibo men therefore are often starting over when they marry. They establish new friendships and learn the rhythm and rituals of the family with whom they are living.

The biggest social event in Shipibo society was a puberty rite, welcoming girls into womanhood. This involved extensive preparations by the parents and relatives of the girls involved and culminated in an elaborate feast. The main beverage served was a fermented manioc drink called *masato*. Special clay vessels were constructed for the fermentation and storage of this drink. Great quantities had to be brewed as the feast often lasted days and sometimes even weeks. Many people attended and all wore their finest garments, especially the women of the family hosting the event. These women often created their finest ceramics for the special occasion.

Clay Creations

Among the Shipibo, it is the women who are the potters and artisans. Shipibo women use a very distinct pattern of geometric lines and designs to decorate their textiles and ceramics. These mazelike arrays of lines and crosses reflect their spiritual beliefs and portray their vision of the Universe. These designs were once used on almost everything created by the Shipibo. Even their bodies were painted with a dark vegetable dye in the same series of figures.

According to their belief Bari, the Sun, and Use, the Moon, had seven children who were the ancestors of all the Amazon's native groups. At

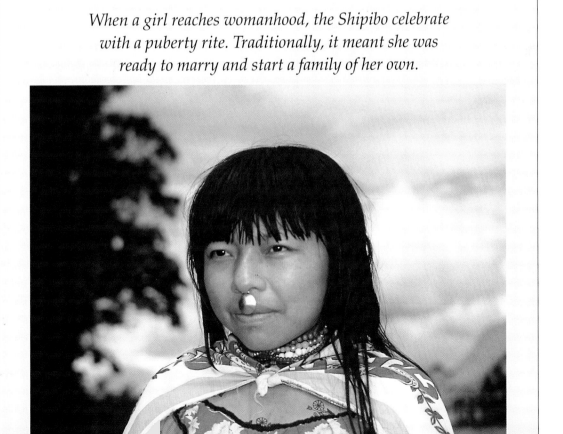

When a girl reaches womanhood, the Shipibo celebrate with a puberty rite. Traditionally, it meant she was ready to marry and start a family of her own.

A Shipibo man (above) wears a fine beaded headdress topped with an egret feather. His traditional Shipibo garment is called a cushma.

A Shipibo woman (left) carefully applies black pigment to a red cloth. In addition to their pottery, the Shipibo are also known for their painted textiles.

the end of their lives, these forefathers were turned into stars. The Shipibo call this group of seven stars Huishmabu. It is a constellation that not only helps them chart the course of the year but is also the source of their geometric designs.

Today this star pattern is seen primarily on cloth and clay vessels. The pottery usually features graceful curving shapes and sometimes includes human faces in the design. These pots are still created today with an ancient but simple technology that involves coils of clay being stacked one atop the other. These coil pots are fashioned by many Amazonian peoples, but few with the enduring beauty of the Shipibo vessels. Pinched and smoothed with the fingers, Shipibo pots are known for being especially light and delicate.

Today, their main means of making money is through the sale of these beautiful handicrafts. Girls are first taught to paint by the age of four, while boys are instructed in making wood toys including dolls, tops, and carved animals. A boy's real education, however, involves learning how to hunt, fish, and gather fruits for the family. Farming, usually using the slash and burn method, is also the man's task. Typical crops include rice, beans, cassava, and cotton. Cattle, first introduced by missionaries, are also often raised in Shipibo communities. The family rarely uses the animals for meat or milk though. They are raised solely to be sold in the marketplace. But cattle are a status symbol, and few communities are able to afford them.

The Shipibo have held on to their traditional ways as much as they can. In truth, today Shipibo life is a blend of modern influences and their own timeless beliefs and customs. Many Shipibo have now accepted Western medicine in treating their ailments. Some groups also own motorboats to collect traditional handicrafts produced by compounds and settlements along the same river. In a dugout canoe, such a trip might take several weeks.

A Yagua girl stands on a fallen log, dwarfed by the banana trees growing near her village.

Chapter Four

THE YAGUA

*T*he Yagua (YAH-wah) Indians are a native people who once inhabited the lowland rain forest found along the Amazon and Napo Rivers in northeastern Peru. They serve as an example of a tribe that has been almost totally acculturated, with fewer than a thousand individuals still living in the traditional way. The influx of Europeans, initially eager to exploit the rubber trade, is the reason for their slow cultural erosion. In 1864, Peru's largest forest city, Iquitos, was established very close to the Yagua homeland. Then beginning in the 1890s, the city experienced an economic boom. Much of the finest rubber latex in the Amazon came from the forested areas surrounding Iquitos and the Colombian city of Leticia, located at the eastern border of Yagua territory. Foreigners swarmed the area eager to turn a profit, and the Yagua began to give in to the pressure and influence of non-native culture. The Yagua have been in close contact with these transplants for so long that their lifestyle and system of beliefs have been greatly altered.

Today, the Yagua dress in Western garb, much like the other people that live along the rivers. They still retain their traditional garments, however, and will put them on for visitors and traders. Men wear skirts made from the fiber of Mauritia palm fiber, while women don simpler skirts usually made of red cotton. Armbands and a small chest coverlet of the same material are also worn, with a headdress often adorning the men. The palm fibers are often dyed a reddish orange color with pigments derived from annatto berries. This same pigment is also applied to their skin as a body paint.

Yagua villages usually consist of seventy to eighty people in less than a dozen houses located a short distance from a river or stream. Hundreds of years ago, the community lived together in a large, beehive-shaped structure called a *maloca*, which was covered with palm leaves. The *maloca* also served as a fortress in case the tribe came under attack. From its protected interior, Yagua men could aim their spears between the leaves at the intruders. The attackers were hard-pressed to wound or kill someone inside.

Today, only men can enter the *maloca*, and it is solely used for religious ceremonies. But the traditional, communal life of the *maloca* reflects Yagua notions of family and community. The Yagua view themselves as a large, extended clan. Each member plays a crucial role, working for the good of the clan and the community.

Yagua men take the lead in providing for their families. Slash and burn agriculture is widely practiced, and skilled anglers test their luck in the fish-filled rivers. But Yagua men are perhaps best known for their talent with the blowgun. With these slim yet effective weapons they hunt monkeys, pacas, sloths, birds, and other small animals. The women prepare the meals and are in charge of running the household.

Yagua must marry outside their own clan. A woman reaches the age of marriage when she is fourteen or fifteen. When a potential match has been arranged, the man comes to live at the home of his prospective wife for about a year. During this time, he works in her family's fields and hunts for them. Usually during this period the woman has a baby. At the end of the year the couple returns to the man's family to live and are considered officially "married." The marriage is then celebrated with a party and feast.

The Yagua believe in a creator, but also in demons and spirits, many of which are linked to forest animals. The most important god or spiritual being is Mayantu. Celebrations honoring Mayantu, in which the god comes down from the sky, are held from time to time. They last for several days and nights and involve much drinking and feasting. During such rituals

*The Yagua considered carefully before choosing a site
for a* maloca. *It needed to be an area concealed by high forest
growth and far from areas prone to flooding. The Yagua
also avoided building near* cochas, *or marshy areas, as they
were breeding grounds for disease-bearing mosquitoes.*

A Yagua boy aquired valuable hunting skills from
his father. While only spears were used in war, blowguns
and poisoned darts were reserved for the pursuit of game.

young children are given a secret name apart from their regular name that is known only to the men. In the case of a person's death, evil spirits are believed to be responsible. If the deceased is an important figure in the community, his entire house and belongings are burned to stop the spread of the malevolent spirits.

The Yagua have been exposed to money but still barter for many of the things they need. Today they have also established a lively trade with neighboring groups and tourists. Handicrafts, generally made by the men, are often exchanged with neighboring groups. They include wood carvings, seed necklaces, dolls, flutes, baskets, and miniature blowguns. Today groups of tourists also make regular treks to trade with native villagers. A lively circular dance often welcomes the newcomers to the Yagua's changing world.

The Yanomami Indians live scattered throughout the borderland of southern Venezuela and northern Brazil. They have survived the challenges of life in the rain forest, much less the pressures of the outside world.

Chapter Five

THE YANOMAMI

T he Yanomami (ee-on-oh-MAH-mee) live in the terra firma forests that blanket the rugged hills of the Guiana Shield, an ancient wall of rock that serves as the northern boundary of the Amazon River basin. Their villages are scattered in the area where the borders of Brazil and southern Venezuela meet, along the mountain range called the Sierra Parima. There the landscape is studded with open savannahs and massive flat-topped rock outcroppings called *tepuís* (tay-poo-EES).

The rugged terrain of their homeland long served to isolate the Yanomami from the outer world. This made their tribe of great interest to anthropologists, for their culture and way of life had stayed seemingly unchanged for hundreds of years. It was not until the 1950s that missionaries in small planes began landing in their territory and establishing the first contact. They found the Yanomami to be one of the few remaining native groups still using stone tools. Today, much has changed. Much of our initial knowledge of the original Yanomami lifestyle has come from the work of cultural anthropologist Napoleon Chagnon. He spent years living with and studying these people.

Communal Living

The members of a Yanomami community live together in a *yano* (ee-ON-oh), which is sometimes called a *shabono*. Although the structure looks like a large communal living space, it actually consists of several adjoining family houses. It is oval in shape with wooden walls around the perimeter made of forest trees. The construction of the outer walls and supporting structures is a community effort. The roof is thatched with leaves, with each family responsible for covering the area over its own house or living area. The central portion of the top of the *yano*'s roof is left open.

An aerial view of a yano. *Trails lead outward to nearby gardens and a water source.*

A typical *yano* houses from fifty to one hundred individuals. Each family has its own cooking fire where its meals are prepared. Hammocks are the main furnishings. They are generally hung beneath the roofed perimeter, near the hearths. All of the ground within the *yano* is cleared and bare, with the center serving as a common area that is also used for celebrations. A *yano* is replaced every few years because either the structure has begun to fall apart or it has become infested with insects. The overlapping palm fronds that form the roof thatch make an excellent hiding place for all kinds of parasites and bloodsucking insects.

The Yanomami are often described as hunter-gatherers, which implies that they obtain mostly wild food from the forest. Although they do hunt and collect the edible plants and fruits of the forest, most of the food they eat is grown in their own gardens. When a village is moved and a new *yano* is built, one of the main considerations in selecting the new site is that it be near an area of forest that is suitable for growing crops.

Clearing trees to make the garden plot is a task for the men. Banana and plantain trees make up more than half the garden. Other favorites include sweet potatoes, cassava, corn, and sweet tropical fruits such as peach palm and papaya. In all, about sixty crops are grown, of which only about twenty are for food. The rest are used for religious rituals, as medicine, or for making the various objects the Yanomami need in their daily lives.

The women are in charge of planting, tending, and harvesting the gardens. The men fish and hunt, often with long bows taller than themselves. Boys are often brought along to learn the difficult skills needed to provide for the family. While girls are still young themselves, they care for their other siblings. As they get older, they are expected to cook, gather firewood, and haul drinking water. When a girl is of an age to marry, the men in the girl's family choose a suitable mate. She has no say in the matter. Often she is promised to a man long before she reaches puberty. In extreme cases, her future husband may help to raise her as a child.

The traditional Yanomami wore little clothing other than a thin wrap

A boy bakes cassava bread on a clay plate over an open fire. The Yanomami grow most of their food in their own gardens.

around their hips. Today, many of the men wear either a type of apron or just shorts. Women wear either a short cotton apron or a wide cotton belt. As with many other native groups, the Yanomami adorn themselves with beads and feathers, especially on festive occasions. Body painting is also common using the plant dyes available from the forest trees and bushes. Additionally, the Yanomami decorate their faces with polished wooden sticks that are pushed through the nose and inserted into the corners of the mouth and the middle of the lower lip. This produces a feline effect where the sticks look like the whiskers of a cat.

At one time the forest fulfilled all the Yanomami's needs. But today, like other native groups in the Amazon, they obtain some goods from the world beyond the forest. Matches, knives, machetes, and aluminum pots are now commonly found among a family's wares. But the non-native world has affected the Yanomami in other ways as well. In 1988, nineteen parcels of land were set aside by the Brazilian government as Yanomami land. These areas fell far short of the size of their vast, original homeland. Other zones nearby were set aside for mining by the *garimpeiros* (gah-reem-PAY-rose), or mestizo gold miners. The idea was to keep the two groups separate, but the plan has not worked. The *garimpeiros* have invaded Yanomami territory on a regular basis, introducing disease and sometimes killing the natives. And this is just one of the threats the Yanomami face. One study has predicted that they will not survive long into the twenty-first century. The Yanomami in Venezuela have received more protection from their country's government, but even there the Yanomami's lifestyle and isolation are being threatened.

For their adornments, the Yanomami have turned to the forests they call home. In several places, the face is pierced with slender sticks. Feathers as well as leaves are often worn around the ears or in the lobes.

Body painting is a common practice for many Amazonian Indians, especially at times of celebration. Here a boy has applied the red dye called achiote to his face.

Chapter Six

TRADITIONAL ARTS

O ne art form practiced by almost all members of the Amazon's tribal communities is body painting. The reasons for tinting the skin, and sometimes the hair, are varied. In warfare, the painting may serve to startle or frighten an enemy. As a practical measure, various pigments and plant extracts act as an insect repellant. But most important perhaps are its social aspects. Body painting is used to beautify the self, to attract a mate, or to mark a position of leadership. It is also an essential part of the preparations for any tribal celebration.

The patterns and designs vary. Some appear to have been painted in an almost haphazard fashion. Others consist of intricate motifs that were applied in a careful and painstaking manner. Pigments may come from a variety of sources, but throughout the Amazon Basin there are two plant dyes that are the most common. These are harvested from the fruits of the annatto bush and the genipap tree.

Annatto is a dye that was once widely used around the world as well as by Amazon natives. Before the creation of the chemical Red Dye Number 3, it was an additive used to give certain foods a red or orange color. It is still used widely throughout Latin America for precisely that purpose. Known as *achiote* in Spanish, the pigment is obtained from a bush or shrub that grows up to 10 feet (3 m) high. Pink flowers cluster at the tips of the branches and eventually soft, spiny seed pods develop. The pods may be dark red or bright yellow and within each are thirty to forty seeds

*Some tribes, such as the Colorado Indians of Ecuador, paint
their hair, or in this case coat it, with a paste of* achiote.

covered with a sticky red material. This substance is the source of the
achiote, or annatto dye. It can be crushed and used immediately or dried
and stored for later use. The men of one native group, the Colorados (*colorado* means "red" in Spanish) use a thick paintlike mixture of *achiote*
paste to cover their short black hair.

Called *huito* in Spanish, the unusual genipap tree grows with its large oval leaves clustered like an umbrella around the end of the narrow trunk. The fruits are at the top among the leaves. Juice is squeezed or pressed from the fruits to make the dye. It can either be used by itself or mixed with charcoal and saliva. Huito is typically painted on the skin with a slender wooden applicator in narrow lines and intricate designs. The skin is stained blue-black from the dye for a period of several days to two weeks.

Featherwork

Living on a continent that has more than 3,000 species of birds, it is not surprising that Amazonian peoples incorporate feathers into the ornaments

In an alternating pattern of black and white, this Karija Indian from Brazil wears a crown of feathers that seems to radiate from his head.

A Kayapó father and son display their delicate parrot feather headdresses. Such elaborate adornments were often worn only during special ceremonies, especially during the Kayapó's name-giving rites.

they wear. The forest offers a plumed palette of colors. Vibrant greens come from the abundant species of Amazon parrots. Striking yellows are provided by oropendalas known for their long, hanging nests. Iridescent blues are found on some of the smaller birds such as the cotingas and hummingbirds. Some of the largest and most impressive works, however, use dozens of long showy macaw feathers. Their tail feathers, sometimes more than 1 foot (0.3 m) long, often serve as the central feathers in a headdress or other piece. They come in a variety of colors including red, blue, green, or yellow, depending on the species. Even spectacular purple feathers are gathered from the giant hyacinth macaw, the Amazon's largest parrot.

Unfortunately, few examples of Amazonian featherwork from the past have survived. The high temperatures and humidity of the Amazon quickly claim the feathers and plant fibers in which they are mounted. Mold, fungus, rot, and insects are additional culprits. Furthermore, many of the pieces were created for specific ceremonies, then discarded afterward. For these reasons few museums have large holdings of tribal art from the Amazon region. Unless the fragile headdresses are saved and preserved, the odds are against their survival.

Feathers were traditionally an eye-catching feature of many Amazonian ceremonies. Native tribes held ceremonies for various reasons. One of the most important was an initiation rite. Practiced by many of the aboriginal groups, it signified the passage of both male and female members of the tribe into adulthood. In some cases, boys were given a test of manhood in which the initiates had to tolerate great pain. The Wayana Indians of Surinam, for example, held an ant shield ceremony. They judged their young men by having live wasps sting their bare skin. The wasps were held in place in special frameworks constructed of plant fibers and decorated with various feathers. If the boys cried out and could not endure the pain of the stings, they failed the test and were not afforded the rights of adults.

Name-giving ceremonies, such as the rites practiced by the Kayapó of Brazil, also demanded spectacular costumes and regalia. In most tribes, it was the men who wore the feathers and played the major roles, dancing in the ceremonies. This was a direct imitation of nature where male birds tend to have the brighter colors and more elaborate plumage in order to attract the females.

Feathers are still used not only in headdresses, but as armbands, headbands, ear tubes, and nose ornaments. They can be used to confer special status as in the garb of a village leader, or they might show that a warrior had killed an enemy. Occasions, such as the rites associated with death, might also require the use of feathered ornaments.

Pottery

Many Amazonian peoples have a long-standing ceramics tradition, making pottery from the raw materials found in the tropical forest. Pottery crafted by the inhabitants of the island of Marajó at the mouth of the Amazon River has been traced back more than three thousand years. Today the Shipibo are considered masters of the art form. Although few tribes have achieved the sophistication that is evident in Shipibo pots and vessels, many groups use similar techniques. Yagua potters employ a method that is practiced by many tribes throughout Amazonia. It is known as the coil pot method.

Any ceramic item starts with one basic material—clay. This is usually dug by hand from areas, such as riverbanks, that may be more than a day's journey from the potter's village. Lumpy masses of the wet clay are wrapped in palm leaves and carried back in fiber baskets. The color and quality of clay varies greatly. Some fine-textured varieties have few impurities and are turned into durable pieces. Other types of clay are less pure and become fragile as they harden. Before the clay is used, it is usually soaked for at least a couple of days, then picked over to remove the larger and more obvious impurities. After it has been cleaned, it is then kneaded like bread dough to make it easier to mold.

Most pure clays will shrink or crack when fired, and therefore must be

Shipibo women are known for their ceramic work. This vessel combines their own unique geometric patterning with a human face.

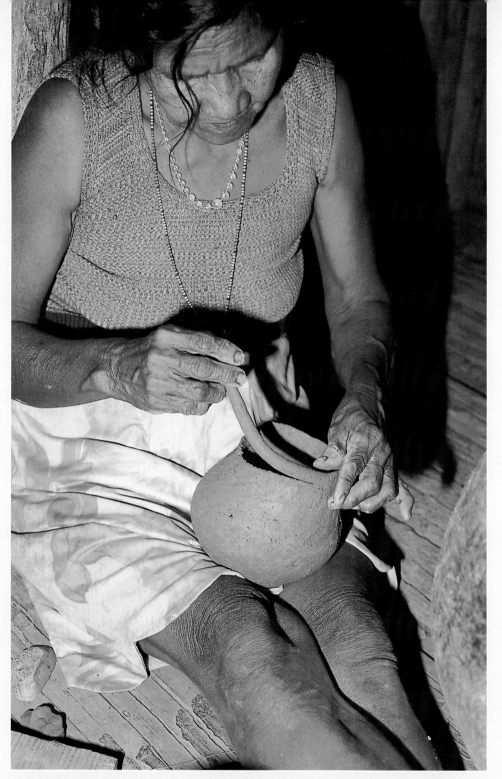

The coil method is a technique that has been used for more than a thousand years. The finished piece is sometimes called a pinch pot.

strengthened in some way before they are used. This process is called tempering. It gets its name from the tempers that are added to the clay. Certain tree barks when burned, crushed to a powder, then sifted, make excellent tempers. Ground-up pieces of broken pots that have already been fired are also used, often along with the tree bark. In areas of the Lower Amazon, freshwater sponges may be collected and burned, their ashes crushed and sifted, then added to the clay. No matter what material is used in tempering, it is ground fine and mixed throughout the clay as consistently as possible to prevent weak spots.

Making a ceramic object begins with a bottom piece of clay that can be either a disk or a tight spiral. With the spiral, a length of clay is rolled out on a flat surface much like cookie dough. It is then coiled in a tight spiral to form the bottom. More clay is rolled out as well and stacked, the first one on the base of the pot and the following ones on top of each other. The bottom edge of the coil is pinched to the top edge of the last coil added. In this way the coils are sealed and stacked higher and higher until the piece is complete. In large pots, the initial portions completed may be allowed to harden before additional coils are added. Thus it may take several sessions, each a few days apart to finish the piece.

Most vessels are scraped smooth and polished during or after the coiling process. A stone or gourd shell is typically used for this, although I have also seen large fish scales and the fibrous outer coating of the manioc root used as well. Once polished, a slip is applied as an undercoating or as a background color. Slip is very finely ground clay mixed with water that is usually applied with a piece of cotton cloth. The slip color depends on what minerals were present in the clay from which it came, and may change somewhat when fired. Ceramics with polychrome designs, such as those of the Shipibo, are painted with more than one color. Delicate motifs are often added with a brush made of tufts of human hair.

Once the vessel has been painted and has dried and hardened for several days to a week, it is heated further by several hours in the sun. It is then put in the smoke over a fire for a short period. Smaller pots are baked in a ceramic, bowl-like support with the bottom removed. The pot is turned upside down then covered with ash to insulate it and provide more even heating. Larger pots are turned over on broken pieces of ceramics that serve as a stand. Wooden planks are then stacked all around it like a tepee until it is completely hidden. The fire is then lit and the planks replaced as they burn for up to an hour, at which point the vessel is removed.

Applying the varnish is the final stage. Varnish is made from a variety of tree saps. Trees are cut or slashed beforehand, and the sap that runs out is collected. Sticky gobs of sap are then gently rubbed over the vessel while it is hot, melting the resin onto the surface of the clay where it coats and seals the pottery.

Basketry

In the modern world we seldom think of baskets as examples of technology, a term we usually reserve for tools and machines. At most we use baskets for carrying things or to decorate our homes. Amazonian Indians, however, have a very different concept of baskets. They see them as functional items that are used in important, and sometimes essential, ways on a daily basis. The many sizes, shapes, styles, and varieties of baskets demonstrate a complex weaving technique. The designs and decorations of baskets often reflect a tribe's specific religious and mythological beliefs. The ability to weave the different types of baskets is a highly esteemed skill.

Basketry, as it refers to tribal artifacts, is not just limited to the rounded or bowl-like objects that typically come to mind. It includes almost anything that involves the plaiting and weaving of plant fibers, and the work can take on many forms.. Serving trays, fish traps, quivers, mats, fire fans, pot stands, ladles, and storage boxes are just some of the items made with great care in order to withstand continued use over a period of months or even years. Yet some burden baskets used to transport food and goods are put together very quickly and simply, whenever and wherever they are needed.

To harden and strengthen their clay creations, many Amazonian artisans simply build a fire. Wood is stacked below and around the clay pot and lit, providing adequate although somewhat uneven heat.

A burden basket, such as this one being used to carry cassava, may be carefully woven or fashioned on the spot when needed. The strap going around the woman's head is called a tump line and makes the load easier to carry.

They may be made from several woven palm fronds or small vines. Burden baskets are often carried on the back with a strap called a tump line that goes around the forehead to help support the weight. Baskets were of great importance to the semi-nomadic peoples of the Amazon Basin. As they moved often, possessions, food, and firewood had to be carried for miles.

The gender of an artist varies from tribe to tribe. In the Yekuana of southern Venezuela, it is the men who make almost all of the baskets, although in most cases it is only the women who use them. For example, due to their simple shape a fire fan is one of the first things Yekuana boys learn how to weave, although it is a tool used by the women while cooking.

The spool-shaped mouthpieces of these blowguns indicate they were made by the Yagua.

Chapter Seven

THE HUNT FOR FOOD

*T*ools and weapons are most commonly used by the men of a tribe. They include bows and arrows, lances and spears, axes, and war clubs. Except for weapons of war, most are used for hunting and fishing or in the case of axes, in clearing garden plots. They are tools that make growing and capturing food possible. One unique weapon used by tropical forest peoples for hunting is the blowgun. The Yagua Indians of northeastern Peru are one of the many tribes that used blowguns for hunting. Today however, many Yagua men own and use shotguns instead. The art of making a blowgun is practiced by only a small number of older Yagua men.

The blowgun is a silent weapon effective in the windless rain forest for a distance of up to 90 feet (27.4 m). Most blowguns are 8 to 10 feet (2.4–3 m) long and cannot be made from just any wood. It takes the strong limbs of the *pucuna caspi,* or blowgun tree. These trees are members of the nutmeg family, with branches that emerge from the trunk at right angles like the spokes of a wheel. When a branch is found that is long, thick, and straight enough, it is cut off and brought back to the village.

Before steel tools were introduced, native people used tools made from materials such as bone or stone. Today, however, almost all tribes have the aid of machetes and knives. They take the long branch and carefully cutting it in half allow it to partially dry. Next, a channel is whittled out of the center of each piece. The two halves are straightened and

*Here, an onlooker has a cloud of sand and shavings blown
into his face. The craftsman pays special attention to his blowgun's
bore, working the barrel and smoothing it until it is straight and even.*

aligned by bending them over a fire. When the two sides fit perfectly together, a tarlike resin is used to bind them together. The two pieces are then wrapped in the thin aerial roots of a forest plant to secure them more tightly. Then additional tar is applied to seal the length of the blowgun.

To shoot accurately, the opening down the center of the blowgun must be absolutely smooth and free of irregularities. The craftsman therefore reams out the channel with a long piece of wood obtained from a *pona* palm. In a process that must be repeated many times, sand is poured in the barrel as a polishing agent, followed by the palm wood piece which is inserted like a ramrod. The rod is thrust in and out of the opening many times, with additional sand added as needed. The result is an extremely smooth and straight bore, or barrel. The mouthpiece is carved from the wood of a tree related to the mulberry and resembles a large spool when completed. It is attached to the barrel and sealed with the same tarlike resin.

As with pottery and basketry, the design and construction of a blowgun provides anthropologists with a "tribal signature." The length of the barrel, the shape and material of the mouthpiece, and the way in which the tar is applied all offer clues as to the tribe of origin. A Shuar blowgun, for example, is almost entirely black because the outside of the barrel is coated with tar. Also, the mouthpiece is small and narrow and made of bone, giving it an entirely different look. So although Amazonian tribes produce many of the same types of objects, they have adapted these art forms to reflect the materials at hand.

The darts fired from the blowgun are split off the leaf stalks of a particular palm. These foot-long splinters are carried in a quiver fashioned from a leaf of the *chonta* palm and are woven together using fiber from the *chambira* palm. *Chambira* fiber is also used to create a small rounded bag that carries the fletching for the darts. Fletching refers to the feathers or material used to help the dart fly more accurately through the air. In the case of the blowgun dart, kapok applied at the base of the dart is used.

This cottony material comes from the inside of the fruits of the ceiba tree, where it normally aids in dispersing the tree's seeds. Ceiba seeds, cushioned in the fluffy kapok, are carried off by the wind when the fruit splits open. A tuft of it is applied, moistened with the lips, and quickly worked into shape by the hunter. The dart is then loaded into the mouth-

*A Yagua man (above)
tests his blowgun outside
his* maloca.

*A cut palm leaf serves as
a quiver to safely house the
poison-tipped darts. Before
they are fired, a wad of
cottonlike kapok fiber —
stored in a gourd or woven
bag — is twisted onto the end
of the dart. Pieces of piranha
jaw are also often attached
to the bag for sharpening
darts while hunting.*

piece and shot with great force and accuracy by a quick exhalation of breath. The point of the dart has been previously sharpened with piranha teeth, which are often kept attached to the small bag of kapok where they can be used when needed.

When a blowgun dart hits its target, it is seldom immediately fatal. Death is caused by *curare*, a poison used to coat the tips of the darts. *Curare* is primarily a plant poison used by Indian groups in northern South America on their arrows and blowgun darts. The contents and preparation of *curare* vary from region to region, and sometimes even from person to person. However, the main botanical ingredients are found in two large rainforest vines.

A typical preparation of *curare* uses the bark, although stems and even seeds are sometimes used as well. The bark is stripped from the source vines, scraped, and pounded. Then it is placed in a rolled palm leaf and water is poured over it. The dark filtered liquid that is collected in a bowl beneath the leaf is heated, cooled, and reheated several times. This causes it to become thick and syrupy. Other botanical and animal additives are often used. Poison taken from the tiny, brightly colored dart-poison frogs is the most common. The tips of the blowgun darts are continually dipped and rolled into the thick, sticky mixture and then set by a fire to dry and harden. Once dry, the darts are kept in a quiver, which like the blowgun reflects a variety of styles depending on the tribe.

Despite the often harmful impact of the outside world, five hundred years of foreign intrusion have done little to weaken the strong bond of family. It is the backbone of native Amazon society.

Chapter Eight

CULTURES IN CHECK

It is an all too familiar story. Long before there are borders, a group of people settles in an area and makes it their home. No proof of ownership is needed. They form families and communities and respect the land that answers practically all of their needs. Centuries pass, and the generations pursue their lives with little interruption or change.

Then new faces arrive. In the case of the Amazon Basin, it is the Spanish and others from European nations who have the technology to cross the ocean in search of new worlds. They come seeking land, resources, and wealth, and the native inhabitants are an unfortunate obstacle in that quest. With their superior forces and powerful weapons, the invaders are hard to turn back. The Shuar, resisting the invasions of the foreigners for centuries, are an exception. Most groups are easily conquered. Too often, they are murdered, enslaved, or rounded up and forced to leave their homelands. They are weakened by disease. The newcomers set off a cycle of abuse, exploitation, and decline.

Some groups have learned to adapt as best they can. They strive to strike a balance between their traditional ways and the modern world that presses in around them. But too often compromise has been forced on them. Shipibo schoolchildren, for example, had to learn in Spanish until the Peruvian government allowed bilingual education in the 1970s. More recently, sawmills have forced their way onto Shipibo lands strip-

While Brazilian officials have ordered the removal of many of the gold miners who have invaded the Yanomami homeland, this native group is still facing an uncertain future. "Without our land, we will lose our heart, our way of living," one Yanomami said.

ping them of the valuable trees. The original owners have been pushed off their holdings, as new industries continue to ignore the natives' ancient land claims. Currently bananas and other fruits are harvested and processed in and near Shipibo lands. This intrusion strips them of an important food source. While the Shipibo once collected fruits from nature, now they are often forced to buy them in the marketplace. Once they had no need for money. Today some Shipibo sell their handicrafts in the cities of Pucallpa, Iquitos, and in nearby towns in order to survive.

Other groups have been forced from their land completely. In the vicinity of Mount Roraima near the border of Venezuela and Brazil, residents have been forced off their land at gunpoint in order to make way for the building of hydroelectric dams. The Wayuu and Yupka of western Venezuela and the Bari in nearby Colombia have lost their home territory to coal mines, oil-drilling operations, and land-hungry farmers and ranchers. The Pemon, who live in the Bolivar state of Venezuela, have been moved several times in the past fifteen years. Their land was first prized for its timber. Today aluminum, steel, and ironworks have been built there.

But what is being done to halt these shocking events? Often the answer is little or nothing. The 1988 Brazilian constitution required that the government set aside 557 protected areas totaling 11 percent of the nation's total area for its more than 320,000 native residents. But politicians and businesspeople believe it is unfair to give these groups—who comprise less than 1 percent of Brazil's population of more than 160 million—so much land, and ignore the terms of the constitution.

As long as the rain forest continues to yield a wealth of resources, its native residents will be relocated or worse. In 1998, in the rain forest of the Upper Orinoco River, Brazilian miners did not even give the Yanomami the choice to leave. They murdered twenty people in their search for the gold the miners believed the land held. This is just one incident in a region plagued by newcomers since the late 1980s. Unless action is taken soon, the chilling prediction that the Yanomami—and other groups equally prey to outsiders—might not survive the century could turn out to be all too true.

GLOSSARY

acculturate: to replace one culture's characteristics with those of another.

achiote: Spanish word for both the red dye produced from the berries of the annatto bush as well as the bush itself.

annatto: a red dye used as body paint throughout the Amazon Basin. Derived from the sticky outer covering of the seeds of the annatto bush (*Bixa orellana*).

anthropologist: a scientist who studies groups of people and the way they live.

chicha: a general term for beer or fermented drinks made by South American natives using either manioc, corn, sugarcane, or various fruits.

coil pot: a ceramic pot made by stacking coils of clay one atop the other, with the last coil being pinched onto the previous one. The finished vessel is smoothed and baked to harden the clay.

conquistador: Spanish word for "conqueror." A term applied to the early Spanish explorers who came to the New World.

curare: a jungle poison made from the bark of a vine, which may also include chemicals extracted from the small, brightly colored dart-posion frogs. It is used by Amazonian natives to coat the tips of their blowgun darts.

garimpeiro: Portuguese word meaning gold miner.

genipap: the rainforest tree that produces the fruit from which the blue-black body paint called *huito* is made.

habitat: the physical place where an organism lives.

huito: the blue-black dye produced from the juice of genipap fruits and used as a body paint.

kapok: an emergent rainforest tree (*Ceiba pentandra*), as well as the silky cottony material produced by the fruits of that tree.

kiln: an oven used for firing or baking clay vessels.

maloca: a large, beehive-shaped structure that once housed Yagua Indian communities, but which now is only used for religious and ceremonial purposes.

manioc: a tropical shrub (*Manihot esculenta*) with large starchy tubers like a potato that are prepared in a variety of ways and eaten.

Marajó: a large island at the mouth of the Amazon River.

masato: a fermented drink made from manioc that is crushed, chewed, and then spit back into a receptacle using the saliva to begin the fermentation process.

Paleo-Indians: groups of hunter-gatherers who originally migrated from Asia thousands of years ago and settled in North and South America.

plaiting: braiding strands of fibers as when making a basket.

plantain: a hard, banana-like fruit that is often cooked and eaten by Amazonian peoples.

pucuna caspi: the tree from which the long barrel of a blowgun is made.

refugia: areas of rain forest that remained intact and continued to exist during the ice ages.

savannah: a tropical grassland with scattered trees.

slash and burn: agricultural method used by Amazonian inhabitants which consists of cutting a section of forest, burning it, and then farming the land that is enriched by the ashes.

slip: a highly diluted clay solution often applied to an unfinished clay vessel.

temper: any substance added to clay to give it strength. In the Amazon, a special type of burnt tree bark is often used.

tepuís: ancient flat-topped mountains located near the border of southeastern Venezuela and Brazil.

terra firma: a type of rain forest that does not undergo seasonal flooding.

tribal signature: a characteristic of a tribe, such as an artifact or a custom, associated most often only with the tribe and which allows it to be identified.

tsantsa: a shrunken head.

tump line: a flat band of material that goes around the forehead and attaches to a basket worn on the back. It helps to support the weight and makes the burden easier to carry.

yano: a large, oval, partially enclosed living structure shared by members of a Yanomami village, also referred to as a *shabono*.

FIND OUT MORE

BOOKS

Abelove, Joan. *Go and Come Back*. New York : DK Publishing, Inc., 1998.

Cunningham, David, and Rand McNally staff. The Rand McNally Children's Atlas of Native Americans. *Native Cultures of North and South America.* Lake Forest, IL: Forest House, 1996.

Lewington, Anna. *What Do We Know about the Amazonian Indians?* New York: Peter Bedrick Books, 1993.

Lucas, Eileen. *Trade.* Native Latin American Cultures series. Vero Beach, FL: Rourke, 1995.

Morrison, Marion. *Indians of the Andes.* Original People series. Vero Beach, FL: Rourke, 1987.

Pirotta, Saviour. *People in the Rain Forest.* Austin, TX: Raintree Steck-Vaughn, 1999.

Schwartz, David M. *Yanomami: People of the Amazon.* New York: Lothrop, 1995.

Sherrow, Victoria. *Daily Customs.* Native Latin American Cultures series. Vero Beach, FL: Rourke, 1996.

Sirimarco, Elizabeth. *Yanomami.* Endangered Cultures series. Mankato, MN: Smart Apple, 1999.

Willis, Terri. *Tribal Rules.* Native Latin American Cultures series. Vero Beach, FL: Rourke, 1995.

WEBSITES

Native American Indian Cultures
http://indian-cultures.com/

Orinoco: Venezuelan Societies
www.orinoco.org/apg/lopeople.asp?lang=en

Peruvian Amazon Indian Institute
www.amazontribes.org/

The Shipibos
www.yolisala.8m.com/shipibos.html

Shuar: Headshrinking
www.head-hunter.com/tsantsa.html

Tsantsa: Shrunken Heads of the Jivaro Indians
www.ci.riverside.ca.us/museum/exhibit/jivaro1.html

The Yagua Indians of the Peruvian Amazon
www.biopark.org/yaguas.html

Yanomami People Threatened
www.stevensonpress.com/people.html

ORGANIZATIONS

Hands around the World
210 Scott Lane
Jonesboro, TN 37659
(423) 753-4319
http://indian-cultures.com

Partners of the Americas
1424 K Street, NW
Washington, D.C. 20005
(202) 628-3300

Summer Institute of Linguistics
7500 West Camp Wisdom Road
Dallas, TX 75236-5626
(214) 709-2404

Potters for Peace
2216 Race Street
Denver, CO 80205
www.cc.cc.ca.us/pfp/index.htm

Proyecto Orinoco
Attn: Lelia Delgado
The Fundación Cisneros
Centro Mozarteum
Colinas de los Caobos
Caracas 1050 Venezuela

COICA
Coordinating Body for the Indigenous
Organizations of the Amazon Basin
Culture, Education and Science Area
Coordinator: Nardo Aloema
Johannes Kingstraat, 7
Rainville – Paramaribo Surinam
www.satnet.net/coica

Instituto Socioambiental
Sede Sao Paulo
Av. Higienópolis
901 Sala 30 Higienópolis
Sao Paulo – CEP: 01238-001
www.isa.org.br

FUNAI
Fundacao Nacional do Indio
(National Foundation of the Indian)
www.funai.gov.br

ABOUT THE AUTHOR

Dr. James L. Castner is a tropical biologist-writer-photographer and adjunct professor of biology at Pittsburg State University. He has traveled throughout the rain forests of South and Central America, but has focused primarily on the Amazon Basin of Peru. His main interest is how insects defend themselves, especially with the use of camouflage and mimicry. His unique photos of rainforest insects have appeared in *National Geographic*, *Natural History*, *International Wildlife*, *Ranger Rick*, and *Kids Discover* magazines.

Dr. Castner has spent the past several years writing books about insects and the rain forest. He often conducts educational workshops and leads students and teachers on visits to the Tropics. As part of his desire to work with younger students, he is completing his secondary certification in science and Spanish. He plans to finish his career teaching a combination of middle school, high school, and college students.

INDEX